W9-BRB-415

COUNTDOWN TO SPACE

GUION BLUFORD
A Space Biography

Laura S. Jeffrey

Series Advisor:
John E. McLeaish
Chief, Public Information Office, retired,
NASA Johnson Space Center

Enslow Publishers, Inc.

44 Fadem Road	PO Box 38
Box 699	Aldershot
Springfield, NJ 07081	Hants GU12 6BP
USA	UK

Library of Congress Cataloging-in-Publication Data

Jeffrey, Laura S.
     Guion Bluford : a space biography / Laura S. Jeffrey.
         p. cm. — (Countdown to space)
     Includes bibliographical references and index.
     Summary: A biography of the first African American astronaut, Guion
 Bluford, Jr., who flew aboard the Challenger space shuttle in 1983.
     ISBN 0-89490-977-0
     1. Bluford, Guion Stewart, 1942– —Juvenile literature. 2. Astronauts—
 United States—Biography—Juvenile literature. 3. Afro-American astronauts—
 Biography—Juvenile literature. [1. Bluford, Guion Stewart, 1942–   .
 2. Astronauts. 3. Afro-Americans—Biography.] I. Title. II. Series.
 TL789.85.B58J44   1998
 629.4'0092—dc21
     [B]   97-25879
                                                                          CIP
                                                                           AC

Printed in the United States of America

10 9 8 7 6 5 4 3 2 1

Illustration Credits: National Aeronautics and Space Administration
(NASA).

Cover Illustration: National Aeronautics and Space Administration
(NASA) (foreground); Raghvendra Sahai and John Trauger (JPL), the
WFPC2 science team, NASA, and AURA/STSCI (background).

CONTENTS

On August 30, 1983, Guion Bluford, Jr., became the first African American to fly into space.

1

Making History

Thousands of people gathered at the Kennedy Space Center in Florida on August 30, 1983. It was about two o'clock in the morning. The skies were pouring rain. Yet the early hour and bad weather did not deter the spectators. They had come to witness a historic occasion. The National Aeronautics and Space Administration (NASA) was about to launch the space shuttle *Challenger.* This was the eighth space shuttle mission. However, it was the first time a shuttle would be launched in the dead of night. All the other shuttle launches had occurred in daylight.

One of *Challenger's* missions was to place a communications and weather satellite into orbit. This satellite was for the government of India. In order for the shuttle crew to put the satellite in its proper position, *Challenger* was taking off from Earth in the dark.

This shuttle flight was historic for another reason. The crew of Dale Gardner, William Thornton, Daniel Brandenstein, and Richard Truly featured a fifth astronaut. He was an African American named Guion (pronounced *Guy-on*) Bluford, Jr. The space program had begun more than twenty years before. In all those years, an African American had never flown into space. Bluford was about to change that.

NASA had planned a big celebration for the occasion. The space agency threw an elaborate party to honor the crew. It also invited African-American teachers, politicians, and celebrities to watch Bluford make history.

The rain finally stopped and the final countdown began. Bluford and his fellow astronauts were inside the shuttle. They had been training several months for this mission. In a few moments, Bluford and the others would begin their exciting trip into space.

As the seconds ticked away, the crowd's excitement grew. At the moment of liftoff, the two solid rocket boosters and external fuel tank would fire together. This would lift the shuttle from Earth. The two solid rocket boosters were located on either side of the huge, orange-colored, external fuel tank. The fuel tank contained more than 500,000 gallons of liquid fuel to fire the shuttle's engines.

T minus nine . . . eight . . . seven . . . six . . . five . . . four . . . three . . . two . . . one . . . blastoff! At 2:32 A.M., *Challenger* lifted off from launchpad 39-A and roared into space. The exhaust flames were so bright that, for a moment, nighttime seemed to turn to daytime.

"This has to be one of the most spectacular things I've ever seen," said John Jacob.[1] Jacob was the president of the National Urban League. He had been invited by NASA to watch the launch.

Daniel Brandenstein was the *Challenger* pilot. After

The space shuttle Challenger *lights up the predawn sky during NASA's first nighttime shuttle launch.*

the launch, he said he felt as though he had been sitting "inside . . . a bonfire."[2]

Bluford later recalled feeling calm and ready. "It was like preparing for an exam," he said. "The better prepared you are, the less frightened you are."[3] Nonetheless, Bluford was thrilled to be in the sky. Not only was he fulfilling a lifelong dream, but he was making history.

The *Challenger*'s trip into space went smoothly. After two minutes, the solid rocket boosters ran out of fuel, as planned. They separated from the shuttle and fell to the ocean on parachutes. (They, like the shuttle, are reusable.) About six minutes later, the external fuel tank had also emptied. It separated from the shuttle. Then it broke into small pieces as it fell back into Earth's atmosphere.

Bluford and the other astronauts spent six days in space. Bluford was one of the crew's three mission specialists. Mission specialists are scientists who conduct experiments aboard the shuttle. They also launch and repair satellites in space.

Bluford and Dale Gardner, another mission specialist, placed India's satellite in orbit on the second day. "The deployment was on time, and the satellite looks good," Bluford reported.[4]

Bluford also performed many experiments. During one experiment, *Challenger* was pointed away from the sun for several hours. This meant that the shuttle was

Television screen image

Crew members on the eighth space shuttle flight are seen on television from space during a phone call from President Reagan. Standing from left to right are William Thornton, Dale Gardner, Richard Truly, and Guion Bluford. Daniel Brandenstein is positioned in front.

exposed to very cold temperatures. The test was to see how the flight deck of the craft would be affected by the extreme cold.

In another experiment, Bluford and the other astronauts used human and animal cells to make drugs that cannot be easily produced on Earth because of gravity. These drugs could one day cure certain diseases.

Bluford tested *Challenger's* fifty-foot mechanical arm. He guided the arm as it picked up an 8,500-pound weight, took it out into space, and brought it back inside the shuttle. This test was important because it showed that the arm could be used to pick up a broken satellite from space. On a later flight, the arm could be used to bring a satellite aboard the shuttle so that astronauts could repair it.

Bluford and the others on *Challenger* helped with medical tests conducted by William Thornton. Thornton was the astronaut-doctor aboard the shuttle.

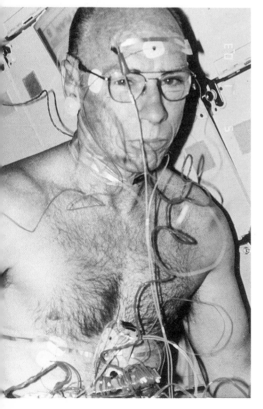

The astronauts wore electrodes on their bodies during an experiment on weightlessness. The electrodes recorded data on how the lack of gravity affects human bodies. Many astronauts have reported feeling ill because of weightlessness. The astronauts hoped that the experiments they performed would help reveal the connection between

Dr. William Thornton undergoes self-conducted medical testing onboard the Challenger.

weightlessness and space sickness. If scientists knew how the lack of gravity affected the human body, they could find ways to make the experience more comfortable for the astronauts.

Challenger returned to Earth shortly after midnight on September 5. It landed at Edwards Air Force Base in California. This was another historic event: It was the first night landing for a space shuttle.

Before Bluford's flight, the Kennedy Space Center had been the scene for many other important occasions. On December 21, 1968, *Apollo 8* was launched. It became the first spacecraft with humans on board to orbit the Moon. *Apollo 11* was launched from Kennedy on July 16, 1969. On July 20, the astronauts of *Apollo 11* became the first people to land on the Moon.

The first space shuttle, *Columbia,* made its historic trip from the Kennedy Space Center in April 1981. This was the first spacecraft that was similar to an airplane, and it could be used again for other spaceflights. On June 18, 1983, astronaut Sally Ride left Kennedy aboard the space shuttle *Challenger.* She became the first American woman in space.

Ten weeks later, Bluford took his turn at becoming a "first." In fact, he asked Ride for advice on how to handle the sudden attention. He had not sought the honor, but he appreciated it. "I look upon my position really as a historic position being the first Black to fly in space," he said. "I hope that other Blacks can look at me and say, 'Hey, he had the opportunity and he was able to succeed in his particular profession, maybe I can do it in my particular profession.'"[5]

The African-American astronaut would go on to make three other spaceflights. His career fulfilled a lifelong dream. From the time he was a little boy growing up in Philadelphia, Pennsylvania, Guion Bluford had a love of flying.

Growing Up

From an early age, Guion Stewart Bluford, Jr., had the "right stuff" to be successful. He was born on November 22, 1942, in Philadelphia, Pennsylvania. His parents, Guion Bluford, Sr., and Lolita Bluford, lived in an integrated, middle-class neighborhood. Guion Jr.—or Guy, for short—was their oldest child. The Blufords had two other sons, Eugene and Kenneth.

Guy's father was a mechanical engineer. His mother was a teacher. They were college graduates, as were Guy's grandparents. Many of Guy's other relatives had become successful in music and journalism, among other professions. In an era of limited opportunities for African Americans, these achievements were remarkable.

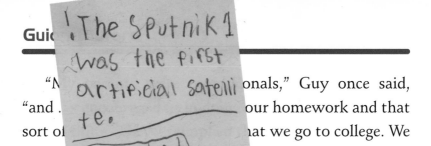

"N   onals," Guy once said, "and   our homework and that sort of   nat we go to college. We were t   llege graduates in my family.

Guy's parents also encouraged their children to work hard. They did not want their sons to use racism as an excuse for failure.

Guy was a quiet child. He enjoyed making model airplanes. At one time, he had a paper route. He also became interested in math and science. "He would sit very quietly until I began asking really hard and challenging questions," one teacher recalled. "Then he would come alive!"[2]

By the time Guy reached high school, a spectacular event helped him decide on a career. In 1957, the Soviets launched *Sputnik 1*. This was the first artificial satellite. Its launching marked the beginning of what became known as the space age. The race was on for the United States to top Russia's achievement. "As early as the ninth grade, I was telling people I wanted to be an aerospace engineer," Guy said.[3] An aerospace engineer designs and builds spacecraft.

In October 1958, NASA was established. Two months later, President Dwight D. Eisenhower announced that NASA was looking for astronauts. The first American astronauts would be selected from among the nation's top military pilots. Eisenhower said this was because these men were accustomed to risking their lives for their country.[4]

More than one hundred military men were chosen to apply for the astronaut program. In April 1959, after many medical, psychological, and intelligence tests, seven were selected. They were Malcolm Scott Carpenter, Leroy Gordon Cooper, John H. Glenn, Virgil I. "Gus" Grissom, Walter M. Schirra, Alan B. Shepard, and Donald K. Slayton. These men became known as the Mercury 7.

Guy followed news of the space race with great interest. He became determined that one day he would help to design the craft that would send American astronauts into space.

The young man soon realized that he would have to work hard to achieve his goals. Good grades did not come easily. He had to study harder than his brothers to get good marks. In fact, a school counselor once suggested that, after high school, Guy go to a trade school. The counselor did not think Guy would be able to handle college. The counselor, of course, would be proven wrong.

In 1960, Bluford graduated from Overbrook Senior High School and entered Pennsylvania State University. He was the only African-American engineering student at the school. He studied hard. He also joined the school's Reserve Officers' Training Corps (ROTC). This program trains students to become military leaders.

Guion knew from the time he was young that he wanted to be involved in the space program. Here, Bluford and Daniel Brandenstein man their stations in a shuttle simulator that creates the actual conditions of being in the space shuttle.

Bluford spent some of his free time with his church group. Yet he remained somewhat in the background. He did not make a name for himself—yet.

Bluford graduated from college in 1964. He earned a bachelor of science degree in aerospace engineering. He also was named a distinguished Air Force ROTC graduate.

While Bluford was in college, he married a fellow

Penn State student. Her first son, Guion Stewart Blu[ford] 964.

After graduation, Blu[ford] While he had been in school, [the war had] begun fighting the Vietnam War. The Air Force needed officers to fly planes. Bluford received pilot training at Williams Air Force Base in Arizona. He earned his pilot's wings in 1965. Also that year, the Blufords' second son, James Trevor, was born.

In 1966, the Air Force sent Bluford to Cam Ranh Bay

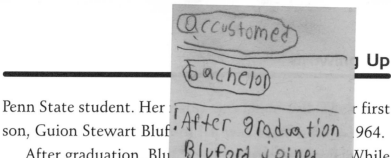

[handwritten notes: accustomed, bachelor, After graduation Bluford joined the air force.]

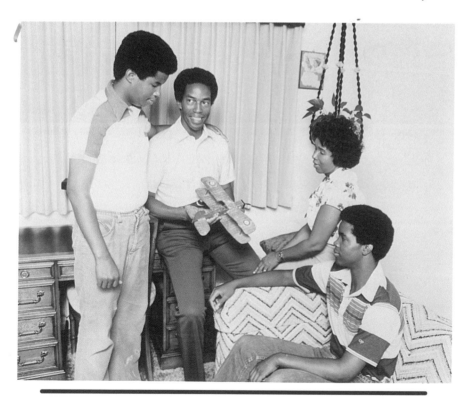

Astronaut Bluford is shown at home with his family. His wife, Linda, and his son, James, are seated. Standing near his father is Guion, III.

in Vietnam. Living conditions were primitive and dangerous. Bluford and the other pilots lived in small huts. They flew one combat mission after another, dropping bombs and napalm (a highly flammable substance) over enemy territory. They dodged gunfire.

From 1966 to 1967, Bluford flew fighter planes on more than one hundred forty combat missions. He was awarded several medals for his heroism.

After his tour of duty in Vietnam ended, Bluford stayed in the military. He taught other pilots at Sheppard Air Force Base in Texas. Later, he supervised engineers who designed aircraft at Wright Patterson Air Force Base in Ohio.

While in the military, Bluford also continued his education at the Air Force Institute of Technology. He earned a master's degree in aerospace engineering in 1974. Four years later, he earned a doctorate degree in aerospace engineering and laser physics.

Meanwhile, the space program was booming. The astronauts aboard *Apollo 8* made the first manned flight around the Moon in 1968. On July 20, 1969, Neil Armstrong and Edwin "Buzz" Aldrin aboard *Apollo 11* became the first humans to land on the Moon. Other Apollo missions followed.

In the 1970s, NASA began developing a space shuttle. Unlike previous spacecraft, the shuttle would be reusable. It would take off like a rocket but return to Earth and land like an airplane. Earlier space capsules used the cushioning of water to land, and "splashed down" into the ocean.

Astronauts would continue Moon exploration. However, the shuttle would also enable them to conduct various experiments in space. They could learn more about other planets and space in general.

So, while NASA still needed experienced pilots to fly the shuttle, the space agency also needed scientists and engineers to launch satellites from the shuttle and perform experiments. These astronauts would be called mission specialists.

In July 1976, NASA began recruiting men and women as astronauts for the space shuttle program. Bluford finally saw a chance to fulfill his dream. He was one of more than three hundred minority applicants. In all, more than eight thousand men and women sent applications to NASA. Each person hoped he or she would be one of the lucky few chosen. Would Bluford make the cut?

3

Becoming an Astronaut

Only a few good men and women fit NASA's requirements. Astronauts must be well-educated and physically fit. They must meet height and weight standards so that they will fit inside the spacecraft. Astronauts must be able to remain calm in stressful situations, work well with others, and learn new jobs quickly.[1]

When the space program began in 1958, women were not allowed to become astronauts. No restrictions existed for African-American men. However, there were very few African Americans working at NASA. In the early 1960s, an African-American pilot named Edward Dwight became a finalist in the astronaut program, but he did not make the final cut. Dwight later became a famous sculptor.[2]

Was racism the reason African Americans had not flown into space? No, according to Guion Bluford. In the past, he said, there had been few blacks who met the requirements to get into the program because NASA only wanted military test pilots. Most of those pilots were white because historically, blacks did not have the educational and training opportunities that whites had.

"But with the development of the space shuttle, [NASA] included mission-specialist astronauts who are engineers, scientists, flight engineers, and so forth," Bluford added. "So that is a step which has given Blacks a better chance to be selected."[3]

Skin color, then, was not important when Bluford applied to become an astronaut. His abilities counted the most. NASA officials quickly learned that

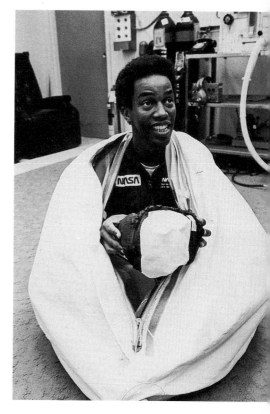

As an astronaut trainee, Guion Bluford tested a personnel rescue enclosure. It was being tested in case crewmen needed to be transported from a disabled space shuttle to a rescue vehicle.

Bluford had what they considered the right stuff. As Bluford himself later said, "I have a strong understanding of aviation, aerodynamics, spacecraft, and flying."[4] Not only that, but he was also calm and healthy. Bluford seemed to be the perfect candidate.

Of the eight thousand candidates who applied, half were disqualified. They did not meet NASA's strict standards. The remaining four thousand candidates were reviewed again. Out of this number, all but two hundred were cut.

NASA sent these finalists to the Johnson Space Center in Houston, Texas. There, they performed various tests. Bluford and two other African Americans, Ronald E. McNair and Frederick D. Gregory, were among the finalists.

Finally, on January 16, 1978, NASA announced the names of thirty-five new astronauts. Bluford was one of them! So were McNair and Gregory. In fact, the group of new astronauts was the largest and most diverse ever.[5] Besides the three African Americans, the group included Sally Ride, Judith Resnik, Shannon Lucid, and three other women. (Ride became the first American woman in space in 1983. Resnik was aboard the space shuttle *Challenger* when it exploded in 1986. She, teacher Christa McAuliffe, and five other astronauts were killed. In 1996, Lucid spent more than six months in space aboard the Russian space station *Mir*, setting an American record.) Ellison Onizuka, an Asian American,

In 1978, NASA announced the new group of astronaut candidates, including twenty-nine men and six women. They were selected to train for future space shuttle flights.

was also one of the new astronauts. (Like Resnik, he was killed in the *Challenger* explosion.)

Bluford, who once described himself as "a warm, quietish person who loves airplanes,"[6] had accomplished something that few other African Americans had. He had become an astronaut!

Bluford moved with his wife and sons to Houston, Texas. In July 1978, he reported to the Johnson Space Center. There, he began a yearlong training program. "It was exciting," Bluford recalled. "We spent a lot of time in classrooms [and went on] a lot of field trips."[7]

The program was very intense. Bluford spent many

hours learning about oceanography, geology, and space navigation. He also learned how to work the shuttle's robotic arm.

Hands-on training was another part of the astronaut program. Bluford rehearsed parachuting to the ground and into the ocean as emergency procedures. He also took practice space walks. In this exercise, Bluford walked around the bottom of a big water tank while wearing a space suit.

Bluford learned about weightlessness in an uncomfortable way. He rode in a large passenger-sized

Astronaut Guion Bluford takes part in water survival training. This prepared him for helicopter retrieval following a parachute landing.

jet, a KC-135, that climbed high into the sky and then dropped very quickly. Astronauts nicknamed this ride the "vomit comet" because it made many of them sick.[8]

Despite the demands of his new job, Bluford loved it. "It really proved to be better than I expected," he said. "It gives me a chance to use all my skills and do something that is pretty exciting." He added, "The job is so fantastic, you don't need a hobby. The hobby is going to work."[9]

In the little free time that he had, Bluford hung out with McNair and Gregory. No one knew who would become the first African American in space. Their unique situation turned the three men into close friends. They supported and encouraged each other.

In August 1979, Bluford finished his training. He was now an official astronaut. Yet Bluford did not know when he would actually fly into space. Many astronauts must wait several years after they finish training before it is their turn to take a space trip.

In the meantime, there was plenty of work to do. NASA launched *Columbia*, the first manned space shuttle, in 1981. There were high hopes for hundreds of launches during the next decade—perhaps as many as one per week.[10] Though this schedule later proved to be unrealistic, many more launches followed. Bluford and the other astronauts were very busy. They tinkered with the shuttle design, performed experiments, and learned how to operate space equipment.

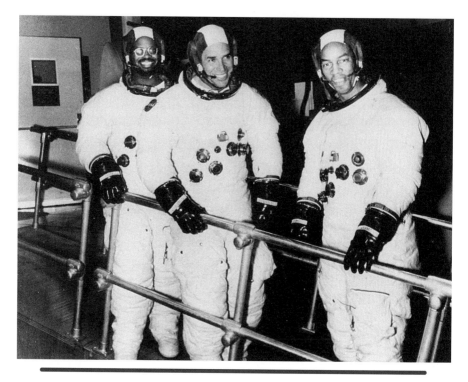

While training for the space shuttle flights, Ronald McNair, Frederick Gregory, and Guion Bluford were often seen together.

Finally, in April 1982, Bluford received some exciting news. He was one of five astronauts scheduled to fly on the third launch of the space shuttle *Challenger*. Bluford realized that he would make history. As usual, he did not make a big deal of it. He simply stayed in his office the rest of the day and kept working.

Bluford did not even call his wife from the office. Instead, he waited until he returned home that evening. Only then did he share the big news: Guy Bluford would be the first African-American astronaut in space.

4

Aboard the Challenger

On August 30, 1983, Guion S. Bluford, Jr., blasted his way into history. He remained calm and cool. "I don't feel any pressure on me," he told reporters shortly before the launch. "I'll go up and do my job as professionally as possible."[1]

Even though he was calm, Bluford recognized his accomplishment and his place in history. "I'm setting the pace, setting the example for those behind me," he said.[2]

Bluford's parents were not at the Kennedy Space Center in Florida to watch the launch. They had died years before. It seemed unfair that the two people who had most encouraged Bluford to succeed would not witness his great accomplishment. After all, Bluford's

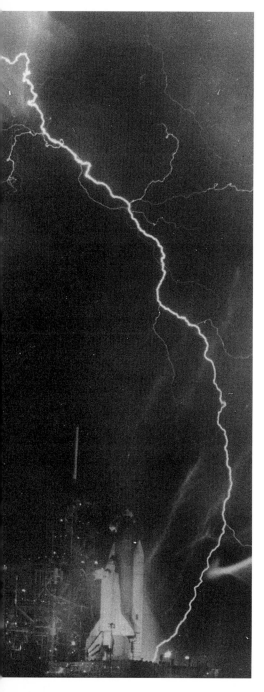

parents were the ones who had told their son to keep trying. They had advised him to ignore racial differences and the bad attitudes of other people.

Other family members, however, were among the crowd at the space center on that momentous day in August. Bluford's wife and children were there. So were his aunt and his brothers Kenneth and Eugene. Kenneth Bluford was proud, though a bit nervous. "I'm waiting to see him go up," he said, "and hope he comes back all right."[3]

Once the *Challenger* was in space, the astronauts went immediately to work. They worked for many hours, usually only stopping to eat

In the hours before Bluford's first trip into space, a powerful electrical storm lights up the sky around the space shuttle Challenger.

Mission specialist Guion Bluford checks one of the control knobs on an in-flight biological experiment.

or sleep. The commander of the five-man crew was Richard Truly. He was making his second trip into space. Bluford and the other astronauts, Dale Gardner, William Thornton, and Daniel Brandenstein, were the "new kids" on the shuttle.

Bluford's main job was to launch the satellite for India. He performed this task on the shuttle's second day in orbit, 185 miles above Earth. Bluford set the satellite spinning outside the shuttle's cargo bay. It spun for about forty-five minutes. Then its rocket boosters fired, and the satellite began to climb. After a week, the satellite reached an altitude of more than twenty-two thousand miles.[4] From there, it collected data for India.

One time during the *Challenger* trip, a smoke alarm went off. Was there a fire aboard the shuttle? Was gas leaking? The crew was concerned. Either situation could have been disastrous. They did not panic but checked the instruments. The astronauts quickly learned that a broken sensor had set off the alarm. The alarm was turned off, and the crew went back to work.

Other than that one problem, the six-day mission was successful. President Ronald Reagan was so pleased with the astronauts' work that he telephoned them. The

The five-member Challenger *crew displays one of the special postal covers that flew with them on the STS-8 flight. This new envelope contains the insignia of the* Challenger *flight.*

The crew of the Challenger *participated in a post-flight telephone conversation with President Ronald Reagan.*

call was relayed to *Challenger* via a ground transmitter in Hawaii. The President congratulated all of the astronauts. He had a special message for Bluford.

"You, I think, are paving the way for many others," the President told Bluford. "You are making it plain we are in an era of brotherhood here in our land."[5]

Richard Truly answered for all the crew members. "We appreciate your taking time to call us," the shuttle commander told Reagan, "and we're very pleased and proud to be here."[6]

On September 5, 1983, shortly after midnight, *Challenger* returned to Earth. Bluford received a hero's welcome. "I'm really humbled tonight to see so many people out here to welcome us back!" Bluford said. "I feel very proud to be a member of this team, and I think we have a tremendous future with the space shuttle—I mean all of us!"[7]

"If I had to invent the first black astronaut, he would be Guy Bluford," said Curtis M. Graves, a NASA official in Washington, D.C. "He is an All-American Black man who is extraordinarily bright, dedicated and possesses strong values. As a role model, you couldn't ask for a better person."[8]

Bluford was asked by several groups to speak about his experiences. Though he enjoyed talking to young people, he remained modest. "If I had been the second or third [African-American astronaut in space], then I probably could have enjoyed it more," he said. "I could return to the society I came out of without someone poking me in the side and saying I was first."[9]

Bluford also received many honors. Kansas City proclaimed August 30, 1983, Guion Bluford Day. Mayor Marion Barry of Washington, D.C., gave Bluford a key to the city. Bluford won *Ebony* magazine's Black Achievement Award in 1983. That same year, he received the Image Award from the National Association for the Advancement of Colored People (NAACP). Later, he was awarded several honorary degrees from colleges and universities throughout the United States.

The 1983 *Challenger* launch was Bluford's first space trip. But it was not his last. He took three other

A life-size mock-up of the Spacelab shows the rotating human chair and overhead storage lockers for experimental equipment.

spaceflights. Altogether, Bluford spent almost seven hundred hours in space.

On October 30, 1985, Bluford was aboard another *Challenger* mission. This one included Spacelab. Spacelab was a special pressurized laboratory where scientists conducted their experiments. It was carried in the shuttle's huge cargo bay, and was connected to the crew compartment by a tunnel. A German research group was in charge of this particular Spacelab mission. The astronauts performed experiments on gravity and communications. Bluford was one of eight astronauts aboard. This was the largest space crew in history.

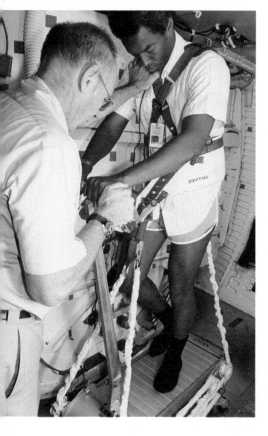

The astronauts conducted several physical fitness tests in space. Onboard the Challenger, *Guion Bluford works out on a treadmill exercising device. Dr. William Thornton monitors his workout.*

In January 1986, the space shuttle *Challenger* exploded seventy-three seconds after launching. All seven crew members aboard were killed. They included Ronald E. McNair and Christa McAuliffe, a civilian schoolteacher. McNair had been the second African American in space. This would have been his second spaceflight.

"We had gotten very comfortable with shuttle launches," Bluford recalled. "By the time *Challenger* flew, shuttle launches had become rather routine. The whole office was not supporting this one flight. We were all spread out, doing other things."[10]

After the explosion, NASA halted all shuttle launches for almost three years. Workers redesigned the space shuttle to make it safer.

Bluford was on a committee that studied the space shuttle and recommended design improvements. Finally, on September 29, 1988, the shuttle program resumed. The redesigned space shuttle, *Discovery*, blasted off.

On April 28, 1991, five years after *Challenger* exploded, Bluford returned to space. He was aboard another flight of the space shuttle *Discovery*. Bluford was one of seven astronauts aboard. They spent eight days in space. The astronauts worked on military

One of Bluford's accomplishments in space as an astronaut included the launching of the Indian National Satellite. Here, the American flag can be seen on the cargo bay of the shuttle. The satellite is about to clear the shuttle, as seen in the top of this photograph.

experiments such as sensor technology. They also practiced deploying and retrieving a satellite.

Bluford's final spaceflight began on December 2, 1992. He was part of a five-astronaut crew. After performing several experiments, they returned to Earth seven days later.

By July 1993, Bluford had reached the rank of colonel in the Air Force. He had spent almost thirty years in the military. Half of that time was with NASA. Bluford announced that he was retiring. In an interview with the author, the former astronaut said, "I enjoyed NASA, but it got to the point where I said, 'I've done it all.' It was time to do something else before I got too old and feeble."[11]

In a press release announcing his departure, Bluford said, "I feel very honored to have served as a NASA astronaut and to have contributed to the success of the space shuttle program. I will miss working with the people . . . and the team spirit and esprit de corps that comes from flying crew members in space."[12]

The space agency was sorry to see Bluford leave, but it wished him well. "Guy will be missed, but he leaves a legacy that is important to NASA and to the nation," said David C. Leestma, NASA's director of flight crew operations. "There are many young people today who have been inspired to pursue careers in science and engineering because of his achievements."[13]

5

A Bright Star

Guion S. Bluford, Jr., retired from NASA in 1993. Then he became an executive with NYMA in Greenbelt, Maryland. This company provides engineering and computer services for government agencies. Its clients include the Department of Defense, the Federal Aviation Administration, and NASA.

After Bluford left the space agency, he spent several months in NYMA's Maryland office. Then he transferred to company offices near Cleveland, Ohio. He lives there today with his wife of more than thirty years. Linda Bluford worked as an accountant during the couple's long marriage. Now she is retired. "She is enjoying the leisure life," Bluford said, laughing.[1]

When he is not working, Bluford enjoys reading,

swimming, jogging, and playing racquetball and handball. He also follows the space program. "I would like to see more black astronauts," Bluford said. "But progress is being made. Right now, [NASA has] three African Americans in the program, and a fourth in training. NASA is working hard to recruit minorities."[2]

Bluford has said that being the first African-American astronaut in space "indicates that opportunities do exist for black youngsters if they work hard and strive to take advantage of those opportunities."[3] He repeats this message often. When the tall, trim man visits schools and universities, he speaks bluntly.

"If you want to succeed, prepare yourself as best you can for whatever career you have chosen to pursue," he has said. "Work hard, dedicate yourselves and make the necessary sacrifices."[4]

"Above all, be diligent ana persistent," he adds. "A lot of times, people give up when they taste a little bit of defeat. But it's important that once you set goals for yourself, you should doggedly pursue them until you achieve them."[5]

Guy Bluford continues to inspire and motivate. The African American once said that, a year after his historic space trip, no one would remember who he was or what he had accomplished.[6] How could anyone forget?

CHRONOLOGY

1942—Guion Stewart Bluford, Jr., born on November 22 in Philadelphia, Pennsylvania.

1957—Soviets launched *Sputnik 1*, the first artificial satellite.

1958—National Aeronautics and Space Administration (NASA) was established.

1959—Seven men were named as America's first astronauts.

1960—Graduated from Overbrook Senior High School; entered Pennsylvania State University.

1964—Graduated from college; married and became a father; joined the Air Force.

1965—Earned pilot's wings; second child was born.

1966—Was sent to Vietnam; flew fighter planes on 144
–1967 combat missions; was awarded several medals for heroism.

1968—Astronauts aboard *Apollo 8* made first manned flight around the Moon.

1969—Neil Armstrong and Buzz Aldrin aboard *Apollo 11* became first humans to land on the Moon.

1974—Earned master's degree in aerospace engineering from the Air Force Institute of Technology.

1976—NASA began recruiting men and women for space shuttle program; Bluford was one of more than eight thousand who applied.

1978—Earned doctorate degree in aerospace engineering and laser physics; chosen as astronaut; reported to the Johnson Space Center in Houston, Texas, for training.

1981—The first space shuttle, *Columbia*, blasted off from the Kennedy Space Center in Florida.

1982—Bluford and four others named as crew members for third launch of the space shuttle *Challenger*.

1983—Became first African American in space as part of a five-person crew aboard the space shuttle *Challenger*.

1985—Made second space shuttle trip as part of an eight-member crew, the largest in history.

1986—Space shuttle *Challenger* exploded shortly after liftoff, killing teacher Christa McAuliffe and six astronauts; shuttle program shut down.

1988—Space shuttle program resumed when *Discovery* lifted off.

1991—Returned to space aboard space shuttle *Discovery*.

1992—Made final spaceflight.

1993—Retired from Air Force and NASA; joined engineering and computer firm.

CHAPTER NOTES

Chapter 1

1. Walter Leavy, "Lt. Col. Guion S. Bluford Jr. Takes . . . A Historic Step into Outer Space," *Ebony*, November 1983, p. 164.

2. Kenneth M. Pierce, "A Bright Star Aloft for NASA," *Time*, September 12, 1983, p. 42.

3. J. Alfred Phelps, *They Had a Dream: The Story of African-American Astronauts* (Novato, Calif.: Presidio Press, 1994), p. 91.

4. Pierce, p. 42.

5. Clarence Waldron, "Guy Bluford: Black Astronaut Makes First Space Mission," *Jet*, September 5, 1983, pp. 21–22.

Chapter 2

1. Clarence Waldron, "Guy Bluford: Black Astronaut Makes First Space Mission," *Jet*, September 5, 1983, p. 24.

2. J. Alfred Phelps, *They Had a Dream: The Story of African-American Astronauts* (Novato, Calif.: Presidio Press, 1994), p. 80.

3. "Space Trio: New Faces Among Shuttle Crew," *Ebony*, March 1979, p. 58.

4. Michael Cassutt, *Who's Who in Space* (New York: Macmillan Publishing Company, 1993), p. 2.

Chapter 3

1. Tom B. Crouch and Barbara Embury, *The Dream Is Alive: A Flight of Discovery Aboard the Space Shuttle* (New York: Harper & Row Publishers, 1990), p. 16.

2. Michael Cassutt, *Who's Who in Space* (New York: Macmillan Publishing Company, 1993), p. 4.

3. Walter Leavy, "Lt. Col. Guion S. Bluford Jr. Takes . . . A Historic Step into Outer Space," *Ebony*, November 1983, p. 168.

4. Ibid., p. 166.

5. Cassutt, p. 7.

6. "Ready for the Next Mission," *Newsweek*, July 4, 1983, p. 69.

7. J. Alfred Phelps, *They Had a Dream: The Story of African-American Astronauts* (Novato, Calif.: Presidio Press, 1994), p. 74.

8. Crouch and Embury, pp. 16–17.

9. "Space Trio: New Faces Among Shuttle Crew," *Ebony*, March 1979, p. 58.

10. Ibid., p. 54.

Chapter 4

1. Clarence Waldron, "Guy Bluford: Black Astronaut Makes First Space Mission," *Jet*, September 5, 1983, p. 21.

2. "Ready for the Next Mission," *Newsweek*, July 4, 1983, p. 69.

3. Waldron, p. 22.

4. Kenneth M. Pierce, "A Bright Star Aloft for NASA," *Time*, September 12, 1983, p. 42.

5. Ibid., p. 43.

6. Ibid.

7. J. Alfred Phelps, *They Had a Dream: The Story of African-American Astronauts* (Novato, Calif.: Presidio Press, 1994), p. 96.

8. Walter Leavy, "Lt. Col. Guion S. Bluford Jr. Takes . . . A Historic Step into Outer Space," *Ebony*, November 1983, p. 170.

9. Ibid., p. 166.

10. Phelps, p. 167.

11. Author's interview with Guion Bluford, October 7, 1996.

12. "Astronaut Guion Bluford Jr. Resigns from NASA to Join Engineering and Computer Firm," *Jet*, July 5, 1993, p. 32.

13. Ibid.

Chapter 5

1. Author's interview with Guion Bluford, October 7, 1996.

2. Ibid.

3. Walter Leavy, "Lt. Col. Guion S. Bluford Jr. Takes . . . A Historic Step into Outer Space," *Ebony*, November 1983, p. 170.

4. Ibid.

5. Ibid.

6. Clarence Waldron, "Guy Bluford: Black Astronaut Makes First Space Mission," *Jet*, September 5, 1983, p. 24.

GLOSSARY

aerospace engineer—A person who designs and builds spacecraft.

cargo bay—The large, middle area of the space shuttle where satellites, scientific equipment, and other cargo can be stored.

civilian—A citizen who is not enlisted in the nation's military.

deploy—To move an object, such as a satellite, into position.

esprit de corps—The general sense of spirit, interests, and responsibilities in a group.

integrated—A society that is equally represented by all races.

Mercury 7—Nickname for the first people chosen to become astronauts. They were Malcolm Scott Carpenter, Leroy Gordon Cooper, John H. Glenn, Virgil I. Grissom, Walter M. Schirra, Alan B. Shepard, and Donald K. Slayton.

mission specialists—Astronauts whose main job is to conduct experiments, launch satellites, and perform space walks. They are also experts in the operation of the space shuttle and work with pilot astronauts to maintain spacecraft and equipment.

NAACP—National Association for the Advancement of Colored People; a United States civil rights organization that works to end discrimination against African Americans and other minority groups.

napalm—A substance that, when added to gasoline and dropped from a plane, bursts, ignites, and splatters to burn a wide area.

NASA—National Aeronautics and Space Administration, which was created in 1958.

orbit—The path of one celestial body or artificial satellite around another.

ROTC—Reserve Officers' Training Corps; a program that trains college students to become military leaders.

satellite—A celestial body or manufactured object that revolves about a planet or other celestial body.

Spacelab—A special research laboratory module where astronauts conduct experiments in space.

space shuttle—The first reusable spacecraft that carries astronauts and equipment into orbit; designed with wings so it can glide back to Earth.

Sputnik 1—The first artificial satellite, launched by the Soviets in 1957.

FURTHER READING

Arnold, H. J. P., ed. *Man in Space: An Illustrated History of Space Flight.* New York: Smithmark Publishers, 1993.

Benson, Kathleen, and Jim Haskins. *Space Challenger: The Story of Guion Bluford.* Minneapolis: The Lerner Group, 1984.

Cassutt, Michael. *Who's Who in Space.* New York: Macmillan Publishing Company, 1993.

Crouch, Tom B., and Barbara Embury. *The Dream Is Alive: A Flight of Discovery Aboard the Space Shuttle.* New York: Harper & Row Publishers, 1990.

McAleer, Neil. *The Omni Space Almanac: A Complete Guide to the Space Age.* Mahwah, N.J.: World Almanac, 1989.

The McGraw-Hill Encyclopedia of Space. Forward by M. Scott Carpenter. New York: McGraw-Hill Book Company, 1967.

Phelps, J. Alfred. *They Had a Dream: The Story of African-American Astronauts.* Novato, Calif.: Presidio Press, 1994.

INDEX